I0760141

raw & zero

raw & zero

imogen smith

Nightboat Books

New York

Printed in the United States

ISBN: 978-1-643-62307-8

Design and typesetting by Kit Schluter
Typeset in Darker Grotesque and EB Garamond

Cover image: alma valdez-garcia in collaboration w readers
& audience at The Lighthouse, Albuquerque, NM, 06/01/25.

Cataloging-in-publication data is available
from the Library of Congress

Nightboat Books
New York
www.nightboat.org

for a free Palestine
from the river to the sea

trans liberation

the memory of
Shuhada' Sadaqat
(Sinéad O'Connor)
&
Cecilia Gentili

my friends

& for you, if you want it

contents

"And what is oblivion's relationship to writing?"

—Jennifer Soong

"the unreachable unbreachable unteachables
hands shoved so deep into pockets
they can feel the next world"

—Wanda Coleman

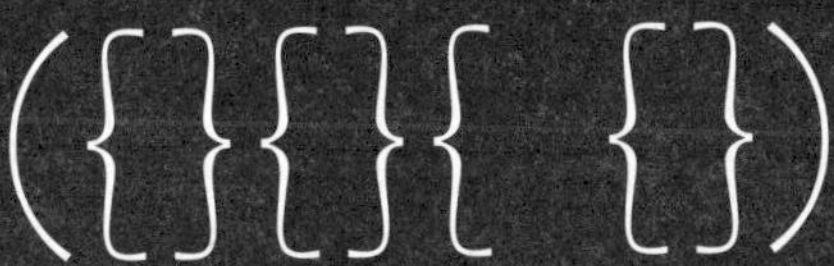

smudge

Movement flutters—

what predictability is not. Outside,
sunlight reigns ambiguous.
You can do that with your life.
Hope toward nothing
but continuance—flux
& reframe. Orbital,
the earth & moon. One
imagines a nucleus, tho
centers elude. For everything
an erotic surface. Today
i pick apple mint
along the roadside.
Despair rattles language
& later, after marking up
paper, after twisting stems
of calendula, i place
my feet in the pond. One day
smudges the next, each
renewed by darkness. Heart
beats break as doors open wide
unto elsewhere. A roundabout,
small town, heavy metropolis
choked in smoke, sky
orange, burning spruce,
lyric sullied,
a paucity of beds.
No future some can see.
Yet witness, in friendship,
the unruliness of

entanglement. Who pays
upon arrival, who child
of extraction, who'll loosen,
let love hasten?
It's beguiling—
truths obvious
the truth, incalculable.
i write to stay living,
read & walk for similar reasons,
yearn for uncontainables
—moonlight
beyond creek slope,
traffic & slow sex,
water softening wood.
The smudge outlasts us.
We tongue & teethe what's holy
& cannot be spelt.

I

the bloodmilk is life is poetry

(after Haley Heyndericks)

i.

i want a garden. Something modest & need not feed the century.
Tomatoes, cuc's, snap peas, melonfruits. Squash, easily grown.
Dip a finger for seedlings in soil. Dip another & surely
as timepass, spring rewraps the skeletal, flogs ass all summer
'till its death red death orange death yellow death crisp death
—ice. Milksour mind 'till light drips thru, finds fleeting soft focus
on the lotus of my skin   ear   nose   prick   anus
perfect holes to hold my sprouting, my 10,000 pisswet wantings—
sapphic mutant cliffcrash, wise & potent. i cry so hard the bitter tastes
ocean, rolls rolls rolls as tides & i turn flipfish, beach whipped
at sunset. Nefarious? Infectious! Gutted dolls subtweet
n' scatter—hot nudes, seven wonders, gay scheming, sowing seed.

ii.

If we're reflections of god & we're lonely, then wtf needs *truth*?
Pilate asks a question & the oracle says *hello*. Mx. Pilate turns sort-of-saint,
poltergeisted by gnosis. i want a garden where everything living twists
beyond me—nouns & pronouns, articles, indefinites, the soil
a richly satanic. Belief? Ambivalence? Skeletal wrap! Life's a wheel
& wood goes soft, turns wormrot, cast mycelial, only not before...
My dreams eavesdrop on poems recited, games of telephone
generationally renewed. Askers of yore, taste my flora—
sassy bitch of fullthroat tease, unseen flowers tonguing toes.
The morning of the poem finds me girldick in hand, ready to piss,
ready to cum, ready to hang there lambsoft in warmwant.
How easily i can love everyone but—   . Some days, forsaken
of grace & healing, depression being absence of all desire.

iii.

Learn to be different every damn time. Coffee up, i come to poem,
sensing fog & fearing—what if nothing grounds me? So i worldbuild
conjunctions, speak motion & scurry to keep up. It's only
movement, only politics & fucks. i want you to write me here,
sex me here, set bones & dress body, lay bulb for frag
ments, enjambements, bluesoak dahlias w their lips together 'n blow.
Guys giving eyes all tough & shit, but in a dreamdyke Leslie
Feinberg-stopping-hir-motorbike-to-fix-you kinda way. Trans
sexual sentences flipflop like fish who came before. Bevies of risk.
i used to think of gardens as drop root voilà, am more & less foolish now.
Love spilt, the bloodmilk is life is poetry.

You must stay open & railable—
don't rain forty days like a sullen god but do it some.

hot muck making

(with alma valdez-garcia)

i.

Come up for air, alma. i'm waiting for you all hot-like, here in my boots on the stoop.

Let's both play into this—open for me & i open, turn me in riverbeds, touch me hard.

Say tie me up in alliteration. Say fuck me to depths only single-cells remember. Say my body is the cave you crave to fissure. Say you'll sharpen your teeth on my haunches, canine my bones 'til

your gut biome bends me back & slaps my ass, tongue twitch toward tunnels, spread for imprints.

Fuck 'till we taproot tap, fuck leather, thorns entangle, fuck to maelstrom, fuck so hard
earth's crust cracks, fuck me amoeba, tether tongue.

ii.

Earth our taproot—logos, signifier, gesturing out to pull forth fluid.
Hydration, a centering circling source. Once opened, ecology shifts.
First narrative—endless, tangled, irrevocably present.

A thru line, manifest malleability of revolutionary creation, let other worlds spill forth
inching away, inching a way.

Imagine for myself a god-thing, the dream-pleasure-memory-quick of coupling. Liquid lashed, i come undone, riverflung washed & woken.
Become entranced & slip away.

Calcify your hauntings, channel leakage, rivulets dragging fingers through clay.

Estuary ecstasy, carve seam in my breast. From (w)holeness & wound, words whisper wants willingly.

Our language—floating like god-thing, breath across the void

always a hole that bends toward darkness. Source of all

this splintering light.

iii.

Earth towers tilling trash, how can we do what we do to air?

What's flying up there? A balloon? A kite? A drone? Us?

Kite peers down through gloaming, sees a beach, sunlit.

Sentimentality saves no soul, but the sun deserves a break from heartache.

What can we say but it's just that simple—.

webbed ecologies of breath

iv.

Accumulating bombless nights, i remember the redwood branch, the olive, in ash, the folding
rows of weeping.

Dear to life, splinters seep memories to soil.

Earth as taproot—private property?

Property, being neither ecologically nor theologically sound.

Fuck 'till we taproot tap, fuck me dancefloor, possible pathways, fuck me chloroplast, fuck so hard
branches snap, fuck me back to single cell, moantether.

Bonelit, body blessed, offer up the non-verbal.

V.

Don’t come at me with your washed sympathies, crushed moon in
mouth. i walk
with my leather coat—wanna take me to the beach?

Liquid lashed—

Wear those tights all you want, they’ll be ripped soon.

Bed of buds, i spread your blood in clumps & q’s, smear my blooming
breasts, middling-aged trans girl sucking you down, mealy metal like
meteor how far how far from source we cum—

We can both play into this. i mean frequencies, amniotic waves,
satiation—beast.

Lithe lovers lick lengths—our bodies, small, illegibly at rest.

Quietude of morning, we pinky pact—if you wake & sleep should keep me,
coddle the flappy fish of my dreams—prayers exhaling sex want in liquid.

Heartthrobbing beatpulse—what a player you are!
Go about yr teasing like it's Thurs night
& you just sent nudes, ring in labret cuz basic

-ally i'm hot for it. Desire—fucking hilarious
consort—push pull jerk jolt pull pull push.
You want someone

so evanescent they blur, the thing about
a crush being implausibility.
There's seldom any follow through

rarely nodal seepage. Who knows? Part the fun
what's obvious is how it becomes you
the sense of you wearing it—shaky

gestures & crumpled speech, a joke in the butt
of yr jeans. My heart digs
the tension of unrequited love

what i call rejection edging—low stakes
heartbreak & flushbreast
distress. You must become adept at

several things at once. What's utopic
about the crush is its ghost veneer, never quite
materializing like you dreamt—

though the prospect contours nanoseconds
vis-à-vis duration. The way crushing starts
is you feel everything excessively

& it overwhelms. Goosebumps as chorus
lifts bridge, when they cross the floor
& you panic, turn beet & spill gut

to friend, yr mesh & slutty
rave gear pierced by wind
blowing any illusion

that March = spring.
There must be a million doors & i
would walk through each of them.

Y'know what i mean? Desire—
too much & always the mood.
My feet beat easy rhythm in NYC noise.

Sometimes i fall in Lissy's arms,
sometimes Lissy falls in mine
or we seek life elsewhere

as want feels right. We always find our ways
out then back again, slightly changed.
Tiana says taking pleasure in one another

's pleasures makes us unfuckwithably hot.
That's called compersion & there's a lot
of softness in the world, even considering—.

A form carries blithely through crowd
musk & yr breathless. A customer steps
up, woos you w their gap tooth.

Taking pictures in East River Park (defunct)
An said he'd had his ass kicked by love.
No joke—that shit'll fuck you up

even in its single-celled congealing form.
When i see my crush i try & play it cool
but mostly it's like the flat

of my stomach's been ripped out
& everything inside me topples
bigass slushpile imogen

drawn & quartered only A) it's cute
& B) almost nobody knows. Only i
can see it, or you or

whoever we're gossiping to.
i like being stripped b/c naked
i am boundless—

i can out-wiggle these cuffs
soldering my issues. When yr naked
nothing about the workweek

makes sense—when i say YES
it means waste me
in the least lucrative way.

Later, upon reflection
there's a subject or several
completely unraveled

—slant quotidian now isn't that hot?
i'm talking about desire
to render what's w/in

w what's emergent in slight dis
-alignment, thereby
sustaining motion.

A crush holds the world in mind
’s eye, let’s you walk
yet never acclimate.

My wh( )les stuffed w paradox
i wanna be pure. That’s a blasé
way of saying contaminated

which is a melodramatic way
of saying all up in it—
crush(ing) velocity, hoarding

new fonts, ways of tucking
in a shirt, bratty little phrases
loose in meter

—love played simple
skip triple poly dutch & try not
to disassociate like rain pouring

from low hanging clouds. One can’t
always be so present—it’s hard
getting anything done & that’s magic.

imagine imogen

Unsure if today begins as i like or as i've chosen, repetition & beat programmed inside that repetition, intercostal muscles between the bars, biting similar bits, durational units of day, architectural blocks mapping my way from digital template to mediums of glass & brick—block shift left block up right avert high octane bike lane look both ways look both sides now says Joni, projections woven through waking—vague reprisals, past decisions echo. Echo. The disorientation of reentry into different modes of material being.

Coffee twice
cereal   greens
open book
my generous bed

Dodie Bellamy's *When the Sick Rule the World* taken a chapter-a-day
& today it's "Rascal Guru." Later (&, i should note, unrelatedly),
i'm naked it's one in afternoon, i squirt lube on my hands they're out for my ass
& it's strange how the squirt head on the lube bottle shines but the sides get dusty,
dust a weird texture on plastic, hands drawn to it fingers pressed
make broad flat tongues fuck around find out   something. The perineum—

it's a forest full
of steam murk mystery
you need a hot implement
you need a torch
go counterclock
one hand now tight
grip throat

brave new world of my glist
    -ening pooling tits & take me

Ignoring what nuance i'm smearing, i'm hell-bent, i'm hey ho let's go, the phone a glory hole, an Alexandria of smut. On screen a doll who can still keep her dick up fucks a femme. It's a cute scenario (not so salacious): i wanted to fuck you at the party last night but my slut of a girlfriend fucked you instead. Oh—then why didn't you say so? You need a good fucking like love my girlfriend but she ain't gonna fuck you like i fuck you. Hands cinch neck, occupational gagging, there are some people can schtick a whole fist in their mise-en-scène.

i am hands
turned tongue
to dildo
pipeline
i am as a girl
obsessed
w squirting

Progesterone gives & gives, sex drive skyhigh, my cock stays hard, my boobs start
dreaming they'll grow old & sag. *Just don't boof it*, doctor says.

Make sure you boof it, 10/10 girlfriends advise

'tho my moods go chop
darkening waters
—look soft but yr sandpaper
look sweet
bitter root
beneath
vibes ancient
all of the all of the earth & earth takes so long to—

i fear my own anger i don't want to fear anger & expect this
a common malady among people, star turn in stymying revolution,
cloistering opposition to (Brando voice) the horror, the horror.
i am a writer i don't want to enact more horror
there is no one thing art is for.

She could use an influx of angst like yeah i'm quite sensitive
but dig it i made 41 & how!

There was a moment, classique, stoned in L.A., izzi's car, we sing
-ing we toking we SUN. i became aware that my forebears cannot
should not cruise where i am cruising, incapable as they are
of homing safer spaces—suburbanite whitehands off clip, ditch post
protestant bank derived woo in La Brea or some pit, sounding in my skull
like a southern family fake ass pineapple welcome ((you fucking faggot)),
they take me nowhere & i'm tired of listening, smoke & mirror
bopping along—don't freeze my tongue i need it i speak &

Knowing the ass tastes sweet is revolution.
Knowing yr own ass tastes sweet kills god & ppl need more of that
obviously.

Pulling the plug a half hour or so later, tip coated with shit,
size of a booger or big toe clip

i bring it to my nose
smell myself
take myself back

in. It's good to know that one's ass smells sweet—as if i'd popped
a fresh bag of soil, savoring a moment the moist before burial,
old familiar darkness rich, watered in moonlight as i do
—anal mystic, transsexual punk goth garden wanting sex witch.
The grave is a door. The grave, sacred. i want to enter & vacate the grave
over & over, make for myself a life of holy dilation, enveloping
moments in whatever duration of time my poetics concurrently hold.

Lazy Friday, Krys sends me a mix—all deep bass kinda psychedelic
R&B shit—
immediately light candles & disrobe, disarm myself & listen. Reader,
no lie,
three songs in i was cumming the hardest i've cum in a year & a half.
Tbh, i text them, *this is the hottest mix anyone's ever made me like*
i squirted.
i fucking squirted. "Still got it" i think, & that's a fraught concept
that nonetheless brings relief. The candles, positioned side by side in a
threesome,
melt to one. Precious image from a soft ass lesbian poem.

i think a lot about how small we are in relation to Everything.
Look at the SUN now see it's all gas—

i reach further
go lower
makes me think slowly
speak slowly
respond care
-fully   sometimes
drag a thought to fray
remember where i'm going
then forget just as fast
i get blasted
i am   much of the time
blasted
& nobody judge 'cause get real
Nobody
All of us
trying to
stay

Tricky little venus,
here's something
you should know
—i am never
the most
liberated girl
in the room.
Sure,
i've slept in
all the right
beds,
floated in
streams
dreaming
life open
like a door
unto
valleyfull.

But
it's hard
to stay
present
out here.
Some days
you can be
yr own
woman
tranny
whomever,
not thinking

twice
but going
about yr
business like
it's all
grace.

Other
days, dis
association
comes like
involuntary
hypnosis
& yr
back at
zero minus
Wellbutrin
& these soft
butch / tulsi
oxymel
tinctures
some
short
kings
gave you
for living
past 40.

Awe
exhausts me.
The seasons
aren't what
they were,
& the city's
melancholic
w shock

ingly few
places
to rest.

There's
genocide
in Palestine,
cops
still exist &
Cecilia Gentili
is dead.

It must be
vibes
or language
or vertical
slabs of air
accumulat
ing the con
sequence
of various,
eternal
now's,
everyone's
skin pressed
from all
directions,
leaving
us shook
& reeling.

Live laugh
love? Well
that's how
the world
ends—ugly

ass throw pil
lows smothering
what's left
of land.
You
gotta turn
yr internal
ized histories
directly
on their flip.
This'll
break you,
& i, for
one, need
to get
broke.

Like i am
so emo
tional y'all—
NYC
a decade in,
four+ years
of Covid,
memories
of breezing
thru places
i'll never
return,
friends lost
to bullets
& powders,
having
their bodies
legislated
away,

the way i
could laugh w
a particular ex
or the sym
biotic aspens
hydrating
each other
—even
the climax
of *Bottoms*
makes me cry.

Tatiana said
something
like "i identify
politically
as a girl" &
of course
so do i.
Cutting.
Vulnerable.
Online.
A flash of blur
mingling
around the out
skirts, always
clocking,
forever
at the mercy
of hulking
forces
lurking
in plain
sight.

If i whisk
away to
the woods,
the woods
may swallow
me. The same
is true
of the city,
but one's
a solitary
immersion
while
the other
necessitates
sociality.
A politics.
A we—how
-ever imperfect—
& i am
nothing
if not
a girl
who loves
love,
the smallest
acts of staying
possible,
continuously
turned on, try
ing at friendship,
feeling bad
about all
the friends
i've failed,
learning how
to fuck,

get fucked,
to really ask
for it, want it
double,
triple,
endless,
& how
that can
devour
or open
you up,
door swung
wide unto
valleyfull.
Let me read
& write, take
depression naps,
be slower
than retail
lines allow.

Try
imagining
a life
practice,
a rager,
the risk
of living,
a rawdogging
spectacular,
sonic sub
frequencies &
suturepoems
preening. i am
awake
durationally, alive

across tenses—
past
continuous
to future
anterior
—it'll all
have been
nothing
babe
unless it's
right now.

In t h i s
now, i'm sitting here
stoned in a slip
listening
to fucking
Mellow Gold,
dreaming
of being
younger &
how hot
cigarettes are.
Right
& wrong
beds surely
await
my titillating
imprint,
& some
days i live
to scandalize
myself.

One
aspires to

kindness
bc the more
at peace
you are,
the more
space
yr able
to hold,
allowing
someone
else a mom
ent's rest.
Maybe
there's
something
petite bourgeois
about kindness,
but we enter
a world
already
moving,
trying
not to be
the fucking
worst.

II

wintersour

God must be passing through me—
i feel so colossally small. Hushed, as when snow falls
& everything shuts the fuck up.

Winter streaks sour   city sky sun-hungry   skin
elms nude along the park

-way. Intersection hosts
maples for modernism's grande design—
plaques for lost trench boys dead a century.

As was / so is—

sickness lurks, bread like chalk, the spit seed,
obsessed w flesh that once went rot around it.

Miracle fleshshroud spin me! Cosmogenic surface over SUNgrown

M O T I O N

linearity breeds a fictive, the gesturesours, w
i
l
t
when subject to definite measure

PALMISTRY
(beautified hands & the hells they make)

BODY
(yoked to UTTERance)

You turn me on i'm an earthslut
earthseed
change is all that. As god passes
through every organ dotes—

in liver, a splotchy baptismal,
as snake handling sphincter sermons
to gush, every heart a tangled *love me do,*
my philandering fascia & warm sack
of spleen, lungs bringing out
-side in the inside, heaving

elastic sciatic cerebral arterial flush

pleasure rings prostatelabiabussyclitbionicaddendums
murking up the

0
0
0
0
0

wh( )le

The god i know exists
as accumulation—all detritus swept together
then

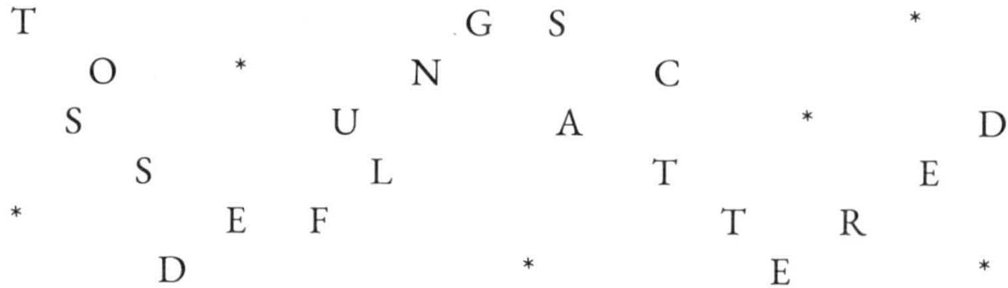

across space.

mindmeofyournameagainyoulooksofamiliarhaven’twemetsomewherebeforedidn’tweonce

witness / reconstitute

Clumps of gas
clots of crimson
& bloodbone molt

congealing beneath the twilit sun

Seeking you —
this side O the doorway
parkway
corium peel

i overcontemplate—all hurt FELT deep w/in,
the struggle squaring thought w FEEL
toothACHE & chalkymouthed

as winter tries our bodies
as if they weren't perishable.

Writing poems is somatic play ({}{}
    -{}{}). i rap at my limits & it's not always

pretty. Words, thrust beyond event
    horizon. Hands beg questions. Alt

vocabulary. Nakedness—
    the final word.

Gets tiring, finding
    new ways of saying. That fucking hurt.

You were hurting a long time.
    Shit sucked & you didn't handle it

well. Messy. Extra.
    Can't even tense it.

Please don't raise yr voice. At me.
    You were sad & sadness lingered.

You were lost in expression
    -ist thickets, branches

clacking above.
    I cried & you were beside me.

There once was a past & in it all
    looked futurefull. Com

-posed of active remembrance—
    biome, full tilt. Ppl mourn

their could-have-beens. It's hard
waking up in the morning. i understand.

i relate. i live w it. Sadness
as much me as jealousy

bitterness, gluten
hostility, corn syrup

envy—voice gorged
on octaves, heart overstuffed

organ & metaphor, what empathy
capable of muster. Tho i should have

softened. Could've softened. Softened.
Soften. They cast not a crumb

of comfort but we get it. Relate.
Walk a sec in shoes. How the body

knows everything but once done
no take backs. No iotas.

Inability to meet
harm(s) survived means

inevitably harming others.
Life slows to a straight line dis

-appearing in normalcy.
Full of can'ts & could nevers.

Boyhood. Manhood. Themhood.
Girl, everything constantly

out of whack. Bimbo
chaos disaster, i collect

years. Childhood here & yonder
where hormones grow breasts

at 40, shift weight around
shift what weighs me

down, like letters
mailed from cells. How

i grow jealous of a lover
's lover. Jealous, having skipped

the banger—the knots & whippings.
You had to be there. Weren't.

Yr scared too, right? Wrong.
Composed. Shiny. Regal in speech &

apparel. Did you see how completely
they ignored her? i felt for.

Hot boy hot car—uncanny machines
their life slouchier. Spoons & spoons.

i want them to notice me. Recall
touch & such. A balcony.

i want them to want me like pop
songs. Here's a mixtape, an ed

-ible in the park. Melody comes &
you drink it up—piss puss spit

in yr mouth, stuff flesh'll do. Water
passed btwn the parched

ribald yet well-meaning
eyeing the ingot, living for fur

hitting every gala yet
dying alone. Who believes it?

Who stays & writes the tale?
Broke rhythms. Inconsistencies.

The body is proof—
a touch biology, co

-quettishly vampy
a dilettante—

verbs & garbage amuck.
Swirl street cluster

i am Collector.
Making poems

my life lights up— bitter
-sweet & hopestrewn

a nude weep godthing ({}{}{}{}).
Pages in a book.

Seated to poem
an act of devotion to the material

world. In silence i am eternal

-ly perturbed. Even the dumb
shit is sacred. Word

—my feelings become public.
Something i said.

Space

to future form
beyond positivism(s).

Here i can surrender
                                        to the movements of my life
              finding the w( )hole
                                  underlying constant

f r a g m e n t a t i o n

i give prayer w attn

to the movements of life

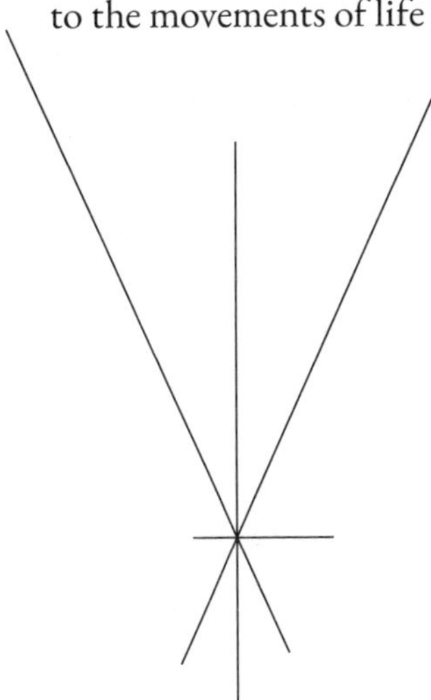

< east west north south material world precise play 'n hot fucking attn >

tissue bones
nervous system brain &
blood vessels sure
to every house room
parcel bite
desire upon more & more & more &
there is Mystery i sense all
about me that is every
-thing plus.

In space there are f r a g m e n t s—

strung out dizzysmut languages

Hear world humming—try & move w the sound

earthhymn   >

< geologic

words congeal   >

< language is

<   as bones are   >

vessels   (((((((((((((((((((((((   )))))))))))))))))))))))   holding

My feelings become public—

an act of devotion to the material world.

Prayer hears everything
ineffable the body already seems
to know. It won't always shift yr breakings
make poems or hours hospitable. Positivity
has its place but the nervous sys
-tem can't always finagle.

wheeling & dealing

reeling & realing

Listening as act of attn.

attn as act of love.

attn >>>> love >>>> beyond the intellectual

maestras
of all things.

i bring my body here

s p r e a d   a c r o s s

lick the cream

& what's up?   THIS—

material   animated w
-/in us   deep
endless   ineffable
realms of desire
for which we might scrawl
fleshwords
w awe—

& to extremes

// /(}{}///<*****>\\\{}{)\ \\
///(}{}///<*****>\\\{}{)\\\
({}{}{}{})

in the center there is
in the center there is
in the center there is
in the center there is
in the center there is
in the center there is
in the center there is

- silence -
root wriggle
ghost plant
pentatonic
baleen
buoyancy
leather
cunt
headstone
dark branche
bull jug
humming
sneering
plastic
kinsmoke
greendark
perfect
ass forever

voicing(s)

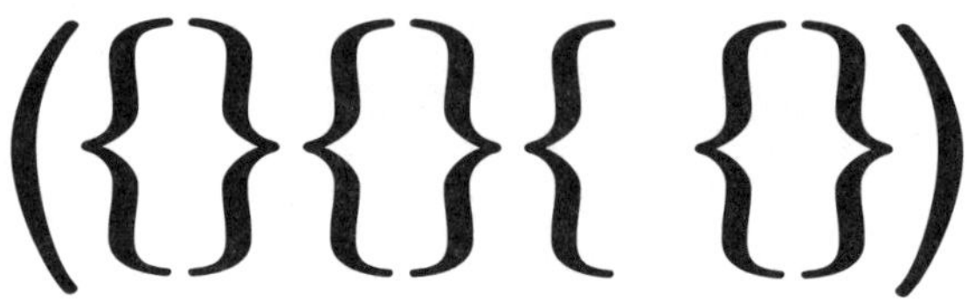

we're here together
humanimal

off center

& holding

tenderbodytenderslapbodyslappainslutprivilegemaimedmiss
-edconnectedestrangement

temporal :::::::: presence

notice
notice
notice
notice
notice
notice
notice
notice
notice
notice

in the center there is
in the center there is
in the center there is
in the center there is
in the center there is
in the center there is
in the center there is

hope.
Word like
a placeholder
neither this nor that
fillable w anything
a form
a power
a name
a definition
a placement
a context
a vibe
intention
a recklessness
desires—

({}{}{}{})

Fair = foul, foul = fair
& here's another thicker than the first.

We (humananimals) suffer
for want of example—

such are the limits
of a normie kinda love.

There's other visions
where ppl

thrive—as in have rice
& something tender

zilch rent & no-cost water
a leaf thru fence hole pressed

to balm. i can almost see me
my loves & lovers

blooming
smashing the menagerie.

- silence -
wriggle
leather
baleen
dark branche
labia
testes
blood vessels
hues of
buoyant
syncopation
mudclay
feline gestures
kinsmoke
in blissed out dark

Can you hear the
Can you hear the
Can you hear the
Can you hear the
Can you hear the
Can you hear the
Can you hear the

// /(}{}///<*****>\\\{}{)\ \\
///(}{}///<*****>\\\{}{)\\\
({}{}{}{})

RedSUN

opensky   thriving

Time is a spiral ◎

i find myself   in the quick

Coffee black & the burnt yellow   juniper   high desert

cenozoic   ~~   rio   ~~   rift

Water tastes turquoise   —   straight from aquifer

i let my guard go unfettered down
the bus lanes, finger the budding grove
this warmflash of seepage in my chest, nipples
hormonal & peeking through stitch.
When the estradiol dropped i immediately
knew—   the immensity
of my own dignity & how this binds me
one to whole.
                    On the other side of the poem
we'll say i fell hard, crushed on myself, flash
-ed a buck tooth helium grin to all The Girls
& true punks in the world, my body more
me & mine, therefore possessing the where
-withal to sway sluttier—ecologically
Kropotkiny, emotionally fuckably sluttier
than it had ever been before.
i ate a bowl of borscht. Three perogies
& a cookie before walking myself home.
Fulton St., Classon, Pacific.

Something loose in my pockets.

Evenings are for sex & soft drugs
a handful of paragraphs written or read
gravitational erotic flotsam between
precarity & nasal swabs   trips
to several pharmacies, markets
bookstore & boo's, the rave in Queens
last Thursday night—all slick
w lube tongue sweat—so rare
's a pleasure, oft guilt in plague times.
Naked in bed, folding my sorrows
listening to Julius Eastman as cars zip
Pacific in pitch. Dream.

We thirst we hum
-man we animal drink light quench
cells i tell the blue-eyed Imam at Dar Al Islam: i am
trans woman thirsting for taqwa

& *what does he make of it all—*

Remember God everyday he says
sunlight spilling through adobe l a t t i c e

Beyond the ridge mesas end
l
e
s
s

sites of indigenous life land land theft atomic
sprawl Guadalupe pueblos ghost presence
ghost—season of the bloodless
blood soaked fiestas

Can a prayer repeated uproot America?

My boots collect an abundance of sand

Light bathes calligraphic—Alhamdulillah

i remember God sunkissed symbiotic

How on distant hills

aspens funnel water

turquoise aquifer

Every
being
exhales
its own

Shahada

III

mutual pleasure mutual

i’m obsessed w redbursts quickening
underbelly, my platelets & poemless
spleen, pinkening fascia bagging up lungs
black hole holy & washed out bones, the self
-contained knowing which is not absolute.

Prax of listening   milk of new mornings
the body’s   molecular   gastro
        oxygen rich perspectives.

To love & be loved, present in multiples
affect & entrails open sourced, body plus people
more people at once. How at once
makes the present stretch outward toward
four great corners as i FEEL myself becoming
part of an organism so much larger than.
        The paradox
being that any *I* gets subsumed or excoriated
redistributed amongst—, but in a way that edges
equilibrium, teases without achieving, begs
a tender tending.

A state names bodies in relation to surveillance.
This apparatus forges desire in the state. A monstrous
reception greets what pegs me. Useless whimsy
beyond a man's watch. These hours worth more
to me than—

If i ask to get fucked
it means i need language   ungagged
imagination until meaning goes deeper d
e   e
p
e
r
deeper deeper deeper deeper deeper deep
-er, not just the matter of words themselves
(though they're material too, inasmuch
as they weld worlds), but to places
we thought irreducible.

i'm asking you to let language evoke through you
become the verb & trust your smarts.

It's true, everything

that is already had its moments
& nothing is new under the

but likewise so that becoming or being is a matter
of perspective—angle shim, a slight jostle in vantage
just a wee bit novel, adding feed to the knew.

Daring desires, i learn to ask for them.
i ask the wind   douse me hot evenings.
i ask izzi if i can kiss them beneath the Myrtle Broadway stop.
i ask the bodega worker to hold a neighbor's keys
& later bring Lis pilfered marigolds. i ask
the missed connection to miss me back
light as the life spooled across hir aging face
(Q train   East River   Manhattan
Hart's Bridge) ask my body to feel a way through
        sentence or line or image sensation
undersurge intention
the possibility of abrasion
a salt excoriation, romance by the by & by.
                                        i ask Erika can we hold hands
on Houston a year after Covid paused what physicality
we knew. i asked the moon last night, coin full
w aries, does rage have an end & if so pain too
cuz manifold forms of ache always soar me
cumming at the tip of forever's lips.

Words are the material shaping objects
that will later be hurled at us.

Us   evokes a many that may

        or may never

                        cohere.

Another question of desire as you & you like it.

Everything thirsty below the sun.

C'mon now—

Save jealousy for pop songs. Boys
w guitars & self-referencing bands. Worms
to the ear tunneling fast about the truck
bed. Blue-pink dawn drunk on drugs
body twenty-two

god damn god damn god damn

the dynamic possibilities
of a grammatically incoherent sen
-tence.

What a long long long

form slippage.

When i tried my hand at heteronormativity
no unhinged happiness could touch me.
What loss we've known.

Look deep

see the moon's empty oceans play earthtide.
Watch pandemic rats strew trash for pig
-eons, pleasuring wormsoil. My love loves
a lover's love   so delicious   i'm ecstatic
residue of breath brought home to revel.

How would i love you if i didn't love your pleasures?

Let me bring marshmallows, bring chocolate & cherries
pool kindling for fires stoking out back.

It's a fantasy where i'm happiest, knowing my friends are
writing &or fucking, publicly fingering
barely knowing one another & still—
adjacent pages, mutual pleasure mutual

sweet onions in the garden

leave it open, imogen

If desire, like politics, death, & pleasure, is always
being learned, then a human body
means everything is questionable. Triggers
such spirit the law reads insufferable.
Who am i if i put nothing on the line in the line.
Leave it open imogen, leave the page go find
the world, cruel & sensual. Any road becomes
exposed, becomes exposition, Jerusalem, a poem
surfeit w yearning. Naming = the first
surveillance—raw & zero, a con
-flagration of warped connection.
Beings suffer for want of fuck all—
such are the limits of imperial grammar.
Suffering is omni. It's hard to see the beat of
stupid joy tap tap to slaughter. Then again,
what's possible? Two bodies, three bodies, a hundred
—mine in yours & yours & holes, spellbound
by spit & undulation. Every switch-
able orifice. Incredible after all, these
things nobody taught me. What revelation
to witness revelation flush another's face.
God, ambivalence—we suffer for want of.
Sinéad says these are dangerous days
if one says what one intends. i say
intifada, i love you, that i want for us
grace. But a poem can't say
what that means.

the sidewalk upshoot

i

Seeds have sociality. The nonhuman world teaches multiple variations of labor.

Poetics of bulbs & seeds—sloppy kiss of iris, precision of tulip—all of it mathematics. Walking thru
the garden on Bergen, i practice scansion. Make language.

Spring thinking.

All beings collectivize to stay alive. This is the starting point of politics.

The city garden is an alchemist. Lead. Sound. Earth. Light. A monument to the hatred of landlords.

ii

"What drives me is baseless & therefore indisputable." That's Elaine Kahn.

i write free new york poetry. Am rendered—complex. Written language generates
deliberate meditations between objects & self.

Perhaps i've a parasocial relationship w humanity, & hence nurture crushes, write poems, perennially.

Dangling carrots of desire facilitate the deep yearning for an eternal way of being that doesn't demise.

Call me a generalist, as in one having multiple affiliations of unfinished emergence. Relations w/out optimism, you might say.

Wherever you rest is an edge. Weeds in the sidewalk upshoot.

iii

Boost the body. The sweetest things still await.

Keep Keats's tragedy at arm's length—as long as possible.

i'm a tranny faggot—yes—but i belong to God. Anyway, what do
humans know
of sacred aberration?

Once, i listened as Fanny Howe read "The Way to Keep Going in
Antarctica" at St. Mark's Church in the Bowery.
Sublimity has touched the surfaces of my life.

i'm a constant student of my own desires. Facing the realities of the finite
universe, do they need or imply direction?

Calendula mugwort yarrow rue.

iv

Colonizers are a brutal bunch by definition. Pillage & pillage & carry on.

A lawn exists to show (off) ownership of space (a lawn creates a concept of "space."). As in *Look! i don't need to grow anything here.*

Domestication & further manicure of plants directs them as beings towards an unintuitive individuality.

On my feed, watching the genocide of Gaza, the colonization of the West Bank, Kashmir, etc.,
i understand the suburbs, their raison d'exister. Make land unlivable. Name streets for what's been

destroyed.

i struggle alongside my friends, my kin. Obsessed w survival & the trick of the thing.

We are looking for holes. Pricks in the fabric. Strings to guide vast lengths of impressions, memories, recipes from generations.

Sweetnesses that won't taste murderous thereafter.

V.

Language bares w it the risk of subjugation, turns bodies into narratives, subject to lexicons of state, asphalt, wire. Even utopia retains a bit of occupation.

What if i touch everything?

Simone Weil might've called this prayer. Does prayer stem from a desire to feel, or know? Why
am i convinced there's a difference?

"Language becomes law when a word holds u in place." Something i read in the Nowadays toilet.

The words of my prayers, my desires, my crushes, will, alongside my body, be crushed by materiality & time—such as they are.

coda

Spring comes & it's raining. Autumn arrives & one clings to fire. Love
travels the length of it.

i thought the liken looked cerebral, venous, 'till touch found it reeflike,
nearly bleached beneath my fingers.

Maybe people are afraid of stepping over the boundaries of whatever
morals have been shoved
down the collective throat. But the thing about stepping over something
arbitrary or protestant or what-have-you, is that liberation is on the
other side, costing nothing but one's fears.

Or perhaps everything.

Entropy, ecstasy, & the holiness of earth. Presumably, there are many
worlds, each retaining their own articulations.

Calendula mugwort yarrow rue.

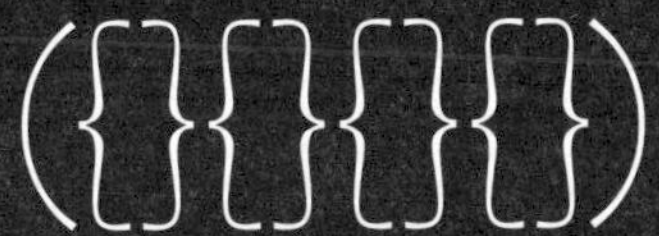

People wake up
in the morning.
Lord knows how
but they do.
i, among them,
take cereal
or blue corn
atole w
coffee, NYC
winter feel
ing all PNW
like wtf?
Only earth
& the mess
we've made
here—white
America,
deranged,
a shady lane
everybody
(supposedly)
wants.

Love lasts
or it doesn't,
vibing along
in overlap
ping velocities,
oft becoming
an existent
more generative

than other
wise known,
given
an aptitude
for slowness
that keeps
the con
versation
growing.

All these ppl,
settings
& notions
to crush on
overwhelm
my sub
jectivity.
Choices &
plenty unbind
the tight knot
ted knots
of me. Here
i am, spilling
out. Scarcity's
a notion
in service
of surveillance—
state daddies,
repro repro
forced famine
abyss.

So i shoplift
affection
from
right & wrong

places,
spit takes
& blink beat
lights, multi
fingered
orgasm app
renticeships—
what i want
in a poem,
what i say
please for
in a fuck.

alma
& i are
always
in the same
place
at the same
time.
Like fate
& destiny, a pass
ionate play.
5th Ave., Bay
Ridge, MTA
readings
riots
stoops—
in them
i trust
my lust.
The world
is not sick
but ppl are,
forced we
of taxonomies,

guts & bones
stewed
for commerce
& account.

Not for no
thing, we fags
leave feels
wherever
we go,
blurred
visions of
corporeal joy
made manifest,
having known
such discrete
violences
borne along
the way.

Digital space
augments
necessary carnal
escapades,
opportunities
to queer
language(s)
w our hot
ass tongues.
This is how
one learns
to locate
one's self,
feeling some
thing's different—
strange &

lacking
words
to name you.
Cruisy angels,
we cum to
gether, moon
circling
earth
circling
sun.

i believe
in the twist
ing, late autumn
roses, that revolution,
like much else,
laughs & flirts,
soaks & coats
everything w
pulse,
blurts total,
unruly
good to see you's,
offers anyone
the chance to be
their best—
which is
precisely
the moment
one's fears
falter.

Outside,
there's an erotics
to the action,
the rally,

the march,
clarity
in unity
as tho god means
“to bloom.”
Hands held,
arms drawn
vertical at
intersections—
traffic block
queer block
red roles
megaphone.
Maybe here,
collectivity
awakens,
material world
smoldering
blithely
about.

Transsexual
—hi. It’s me,
imogen,
present,
knowing
everything’s
alive, thus
mutably
complex.
This path
i choose,
become strange
& connect,
surrender to,
bearing it

whole,
up & down
the avenues,
everywhere
my body
goes.

With me,
babe, it's all
alluvial.
Categorical
refusal, trans
sexual liminal—
spiritual acts.
The place where
remaining &
staying possible,
where showing
up, touching
the riot,
hearing the riot
& witnessing
the mess
makes sense.
It's like
intuition +
risk = love
& nothing's
ever been
clearer:

same soul
everywhere.

My Loves
& i? We fist

suck & cuddle,
curtains drawn
wide for a Bed-
Stuy street,
breathless
as the west
unravels.

Fucking,
getting fucked,
Adderall,
really any up
per, a tulsi
spliff to close
the night.
i was a drunk,
turned
sober,
now laugh
in the middle—
whatever.
Genealogies, all
my selfish acts,
my quasi self
less gesturings,
the ability
to hold
you
& them
& them.
These things
& others
—friends,
lovers, punk
shows in parks,
my crush,

my crushes,
the hopes
i hold for my
self, some sort of
ethics derived
partially
on the spot,
a free Palestine
/ queer liberation,
the twist
the tutti frutti
shahada
the softening
toward—
all of this
will have
pulled me
through. Various
failures. Num
erous, gaudy
ruins,
an adorably
stupid girl
living &
dying
in
America.

Hello

notes

I get the feeling that a defining subject of poetry is often, more or less, poetry. With that said, the poems herein exist in conversation with so many artists across space, time, & medium. *raw & zero* entered the world in an epoch of pandemic, genocide, mass war, poverty, corruption, & environmental destruction. Thus, the pieces are not neutral—their breadth, scope, & usefulness (or lack thereof) exists in proportion to their author's ability to witness herself, their conditions, their moment, & offer response in good faith.

Epigraphs come from Jennifer Soong's *Slips of the Mind* (2025), & the poem "Los Angeles Nocturne" in Wanda Coleman's *Ostinato Vamps* (2003).

"smudge" references a NYC drenched in orange-gray smoke & haze, as these elements traveled southward from the Canadian wildfires of summer, 2023.

The line "i want a garden," referencing Haley Heyndericks's song "Oom Sha La La" from the album *I Need to Start a Garden*, served as the starting point for "the bloodmilk...". Mx. Pilate—she who had prophetic dreams of Jesus' innocence—can be found in the distant annals of Christendom. Leslie Feinberg was a self-described "anti-racist white, working-class, secular Jewish, transgender, lesbian, female revolutionary communist."

"hot muckmaking" was co-written with alma valdez-garcia between 2023-24. Nothing makes sense like collaboration!

"the parasocialites" liberally quotes several friends, & owes its entire existence to Tiana Reid, as well as Tiana's "Crush Redux" class i took in 2021 through The Poetry Project.

Make sure you boof it, 10/10 girlfriends advise.

At some point, monti & i were talking & they said "tricky little venus." Thanks monti, for the title+ <3. Cecilia Gentili is a saint & Mother of so many trans women who endure due to her legacy for transsexuals & sex workers. She was a friend of mine & i will never forget our sweet moments of laughter & knowing—CECILIA!!! *Bottoms* (2023) is a comedy film by Emma Seligman i wish i'd had as a child, & *Mellow Gold* (1994) is an album by Beck.

"wintersour's" trench boys reference a monument to NYC's soldiers of "the great war."

The symbol ({}{}{}{}) first appears in "collector," & takes various shapes across the book. It is my symbol for God, the Divine, cosmos, consciousness, something totally unutterable. A somewhat similar symbol, availed for different contexts, appears in Sarah Sgro's book *If The Future Is A Fetish.*

"Fair = foul" is a riff on the witches of Macbeth.

At Abiquiú, i had the privilege to visit some of the congregants, as well as the Imam, of Dar Al-Islam, an enormous & ornate adobe Masjid. Big thanks to the gracious women i met there, as well as the Imam who offered this advice to a transsexual revert: "remember God every day."

"leave it open, imogen" references Sinéad O'Connor's song "Black Boys on Mopeds" from her album *I Do Not Want What I Haven't Got* (1990).

Fanny Howe read Bernadette Mayer's poem "The Way to Keep Going in Antarctica" at Bernadette's memorial celebration at The Poetry Project, May 12, 2023.

Nowadays is a club in Ridgewood, Queens.

"Presumably, there are many worlds..." is a riff on and reference to The Holy Qur'an. "Calendula mugwort yarrow rue" refers to the contents of my portable altar, culled together in alma valdez-garcia's Field Meridians workshop, "Ecopoetics as Ritual, Part I" (April, 2024).

The line "a shady lane / everybody / ... / wants" comes from the song "Shady Lane" by Pavement, from their 1997 record *Brighten the Corners* (the "(supposedly)" is my own addition). I often think of a James Baldwin quote from Raoul Peck's film *I Am Not Your Negro*, in which Baldwin says—i'm paraphrasing—something to the effect of white ppl need to realize that their house & yard & picket fence comes at the expense of the death of the world.

acknowledgements

Bismallah,

A book, being the sum total of all engagements informing it, is only as good as the conversations & work it holds capacity to inspire. In other words, I am everlastingly grateful to the communities & contexts which make, undo, & remake me.

I began writing these poems in January, 2022, under the tutelage of Stacy Szymaszek, as an Emerge-Surface-Be Fellow at The Poetry Project. Stacy—thank you for encouraging me as a reader, worker, & experimenter as this work took shape.

Alisha Mascarenhas was the first reader of many of these pieces, & I am gratefully in awe of your discursive intellect, mutual engagement, & search for spiritual groundedness. May we continue taking risks together.

Jaye Elizabeth Elijah gave *raw & zero* its first editorial pass, pushing me to clarify, cut, think, & rethink these pieces. Your brain, thoughtfulness, & humor provided immense grounding & seismic shifts—w my whole heart, i can't thank you enough.

Infinite thanks & love to alma valdez-garcia, my boo & collaborator, w/out whose affirmations, edits, solidarity, support, & overall belief in me (beyond any work) is the thread holding these poems together. Thank you for showing me more care than i know what to do w!

Jazakallah: a.Monti, Alisha Mascarenhas, Alexander Dwinell, alma valdez-garcia, An Duplan, Angelique Rosales Salgado, arianne ayu alizio, Aristilde Kirby, Bahaar Ahsan, CAConrad, Callen, Caitlin Lynch, Camille Roy, Cecilia Gentili, Cerine Z, Cookie Hagendorf, Dr. Cornel

West, David Glickman, Deepali Zeer, Emily Lee Luan, Emji Saint Spero, Ely Watson, Erica Dawn Lyle, Erika Hodges, Evan Kennedy, Forrest Gray Yerman, Garrett Phelps, Ian Burke, Ivanna Baranova, Ivy Johnson, izzi rojas, James Barickman, Jamie Townsend, Jaye Elizabeth Elijah, Dr. Jerusha Rhodes, Julian Talamantez Brolaski, Kerosene Jones, Krys, Laura Henriksen, Lindsay Dula, Lissy Navantu, Mallika Singh, marcus scott williams, Malvika Jolly, Miguel Gutierrez, Mohammed Zenia Siddiq Yusef Ibrahim, Mónica de la Torre, Morgan Võ, Nancy Huang, Naima Yael Tokunow, Nm Esc, Noah Ross, Ollie Hunt, Peach Kander, Rebecca Teich, Rider Alsop, Rosie Stockton, Sarah Aziza, Sarah Jane Stoner, sarah sao mai habib, Sarah Steadman, Seth Sullivan, Sheridan Riley, Sol Cabrini, Sophia Dahlin, Stories Books, Suzanne Goldenberg, Tassja Walker, Tatiana Luboviski-Acosta, Tess Brown-Lavoie, Tom Lloyd, Trish Salah, Unnameable Books, Violet Spurlock, Wo Chan, The Word Is Change, Zefyr Lisowski, & everyone who has supported me, in one way or another, over the last few years.

Alf Shukr to The Poetry Project, Blue Mountain Center, Mount Lebanon Residency, Brooklyn Poets, The New York Foundation for the Arts, Al-Wasi Collective, my peers at Union Theological Seminary, Poetic Research Bureau, & everyone who hosted / came out for EDL & i's "Emotional Labor Tour" in 2023, for communal, institutional, financial, & spiritual support.

It's such an honor having dreamy-ass Nightboat Books usher this project into the world! No thanks is enough thanks for Stephen Motika, Emily Bark Brown (your editing keeps me humble!), Lina Bergamini (for literally everything), Lindsey Boldt, Morgan Levine, Kit Schluter, & Dante Silva. Thanks for your friendship, patience, guidance, & care in helping me see this project through. So blessed to be part of this family!

Thanks to the editors of *Baest*, *Big Bell*, *Folder*, *Hot Pink Mag*, *Poetry Foundation*, *The Poetry Project Newsletter*, *The Recluse*, *The Southeastern Review*, & *Swan's Rag*, where several of these poems first appeared, often in radically different form.

To my friends Aristilde Kirby, Evan Kennedy, Nat Raha, Tatiana Luboviski-Acosta, & Julian Talamantez Brolaski, i adore y'all & live for your work—thank you for the kindest of blurbs...y'all got me blushing, eternally!

raw & zero was written between 2022—2024, mostly in Crown Heights, Brooklyn, while also touching earth in the Adirondacks & New Lebanon, NY, New Mexico, and Los Angeles, CA. Thank you to everyone who hosted, booked me, attended a reading, & shared so much of yourselves (especially every transsexual) w me—what is this thing, poetry, that binds us together w such heart?!

While writing this text, i was guided, inspired, obsessed, with the work of Ana Mendieta, Beach House, Clarice Lispector, Mei-mei Berssenbrugge, N.H. Pritchard, Simone Weil, Sineád O'Connor, *Women in Concrete Poetry: 1959-1979*, the movement for Palestinian Liberation, a whole slew of radical queers, and The Holy Qur'an.

To all artists & arts organizations: have you not already done so, please join the BDS movement, sign on to PACBI, & support liberation movements everywhere, with whatever means available, & all the passion you have to offer.

A final thanks again to alma, & to God, the All Merciful, Ever Merciful—Alhamdulillah!

imogen smith is a poet and transsexual. She is the author of *stemmy things*, also from Nightboat Books. Her writings have appeared in this journal and that, and she is the recipient of fellowships from The Poetry Project and NYFA. imogen loves true punks, hates cops of all denominations, and believes in a free Palestine.

Nightboat Books

Nightboat Books, a nonprofit organization, seeks to develop audiences for writers whose work resists convention and transcends boundaries. We publish books rich with poignancy, intelligence, and risk. Please visit nightboat.org to learn about our titles and how you can support our future publications.

The following individuals have supported the publication of this book. We thank them for their generosity and commitment to the mission of Nightboat Books:

Kazim Ali, Anonymous (3), Ava Aviva Avnisan, Jean C. Ballantyne, Rumeli Banik, Will Blythe, Rob Byrnes, V. Shannon Clyne, Theodore Cornwell, Gisela Gamper, Photios Giovanis, Amanda Greenberger, David Groff, Jonathan Groff, Daniel Handler, Sarah Heller, Karen Holtzman, Parag Rajendra Khandhar, Katy Lederer, Shari Leinwand, Daniel Levine, Elizabeth Madans, Ricardo Maldonado, Pooja Mehta, Ethan Mitchell, Caren Motika, Elizabeth Motika, Asker Saeed, The Leslie Scalapino - O Books Fund, Amy Scholder, Eric Suchyta, Benjamin Taylor, Mohan Trivedi, Divya Victor, Jerrie Whitfield & Richard Motika, Clay Williams

This book is made possible, in part, by grants from the New York City Department of Cultural Affairs in partnership with the City Council and the New York State Council on the Arts Literature Program.

www.ingramcontent.com/pod-product-compliance
Lightning Source LLC
LaVergne TN
LVHW010937100826
845153LV00001B/73
9781946767066